Out of the Darkness and Into the Light

Out of the Darkness and Into the Light

My Personal Struggle with Schizoaffective Disorder and How the Illness Brought me Closer to God

By

Lora Bell

© Copyright 2011, Lora Bell

All Rights Reserved.

No part of this book may be reproduced, stored in a retrieval system, or transmitted by any means, electronic, mechanical, photocopying, recording, or otherwise, without written permission from the author.

ISBN: 978-1-936750-20-7

This book is dedicated to the memory of John, my father-in-law, who loved and supported me through my illness. He will be truly missed.

Acknowledgements

I have written this book in the hope that my story will help others who struggle with mental illness. I hope that they will learn something about their own lives and thus consider the question of whether they need to change how they are living. There is so much that is unknown about mental illness, due in part to there being no physical cause to the disease. To me, this leaves many unanswered questions about what causes people to become mentally ill.

I thank God, who kept me alive when there were so many times I felt I could have died. He gave me the strength to keep going and the ability to recall all my experiences in great detail. He wanted me to write my story to help others who struggle with their personal demons, and I can only hope my book finds them.

I would like to thank my family for supporting me through my horrible history of illness and for being there for me during each and every hospital visit. Thank you, David, for staying by my side through all these ups and downs this illness has brought to us. I know we have struggled through many hospital visits and some postpartum problems after our second child was born, but I know all of it was worth it. We have three beautiful, healthy daughters and I feel I am more stable and at peace than ever because of my decision to become a Christian. I thank you for convincing me that becoming a Christian was the right thing to do with my life.

Thank you, Mom, for traveling from Pennsylvania many times and staying with us while I was sick. You were a huge help to David and me through the years and we so appreciate it. You supported me and believed in me, and for that I will always love you.

Thank you, Sue, my mother-in-law, for helping out during the many times I was in the hospital or came close to being hospitalized. You were also a help to David and me.

Thank you, Carrie, for being a sister-in-law and friend. I could always count on you when I needed you the most. You helped me through many tough times and answered a lot of my questions about becoming a Christian.

Thank you, Julie, for convincing me that I needed to wait no longer to get baptized. You helped answer a lot of questions I had about religion and will always be one of my true friends.

I thank Nicole and also David Bagdade for helping me edit my book and for answering questions about publishing.

Contents

Foreword xi

Introduction xv

One
The Wedding 1

Two
Second Hospitalization 5

Three
The Pregnancy 7

Four
My World is Coming to an End 9

Five
Move to Indianapolis 12

Six
Another Baby? 17

Seven
Religion Problems 21

Eight
Christmas in Indianapolis 25

Nine
My Condition Gets Worse..30

Ten
Hospital Stay 34

Eleven
An End in Sight..45

Twelve
A Story of Hope 48

Thirteen
Could Satan Contribute to Illness? 51

Fourteen
What Do You Have To Do To Become a Christian.......................53

Foreword

Out of the Darkness and Into the Light is an amazing and inspiring book written by a young Christian woman who has devoted her life to God. This book provides a brief but intimate look into the struggles she encountered before she became a Christian and was baptized into the Lord. This telling and personal autobiography also reaches out to all individuals who live with schizoaffective disorder, assuring them that they are not alone, that there are others out there experiencing the same hardships, and, most importantly, letting them know God will see them through. The author has dedicated a year of her life to sharing her special story about how God has blessed her and changed her life forever.

I had the wonderful privilege to witness the baptism of Lora Bell, and it filled me with so many positive emotions to know that this young woman has made the commitment to become a child of God. It was so encouraging and uplifting to me and it inspired me to work harder as a Christian to spread the truth of God's word and grow the Lord's church. At that time, Lora and I had known each other for approximately one year, during which time we had grown closer and become good friends. We had attended ladies' Bible classes together, arranged play-dates with our small children, organized family gatherings and, of course, worshiped together three times a week at church services. Over time, she shared with me her personal experiences with schizoaffective disorder and how she dealt with the darkness and the helplessness of the experiences she felt while being admitted to the hospital. Thankfully, she was blessed with her own angel on earth, her husband David, who loved her unconditionally each time she had to be admitted.

The very best part of this book is the message that there truly is a light at the end of the tunnel. Lora has exposed her own personal miseries and extreme vulnerabilities in this autobiography so as to benefit all individuals who have endured similar hardships so they will know Jesus loves them and He can help them come out from the darkness and into the light. The benefit is that the reader gets a glimpse of the big picture, seeing through the lens at all angles. Lora has successfully worked through her own difficulties. She has independently studied schizoaffective disorder and survived experiences in and out of the hospital. You will learn about schizoaffective disorder, its early signs and symptoms and treatment options, all of which enable you in aiding a loved one to conquer this mystifying disease.

This autobiography is important to me because I see it as an opportunity for every one of us to evaluate our own lives, appreciate our many blessings and discover how we too can give back to God. I challenge you to read this book and assess your own existence and how you can become a child of God, to reach out to others in need and assist them in learning the truth. With prayer, study and full immersion baptism, this commitment to God can forever bring you out of the darkness and into the light.

——Julie
Close friend of Lora Bell

Author's Note

All names have been changed to protect the identity of the individuals in this book, including the author's name. The hospital names and doctor's names have also been changed. In addition, some locations and dates have been altered.

Introduction

I remember the day rather vividly. I had just been admitted to the psychiatric ward for my fourth hospitalization. We were having a meeting with my family and some of the hospital staff. I sat there drugged out on the medicines. I listened as the nurses and doctors all agreed that I had a serious mental illness and that I would probably be in and out of hospital psychiatric wards all my life. The reality of the meeting did not really sink in. I was just starting out my life. I was in my early twenties, newly married with a 6-month-old. How was I going to live a normal life?

My name is Lora Bell, and I have struggled with schizoaffective disorder since October of 1997. I finally see a light at the end of the tunnel of my disorder since I became a Christian in 2009 after a horrible experience in a mental hospital. The reason why I am writing this book is because God has helped me. I feel that, now that I am a Christian, my disorder is under control. I still need my medicine, but I feel I will never have another psychotic break again. I want to share my experiences with others who have mental illness and let them know that they are not alone. I have this mental illness, but it does not stop me from leading a normal life. I have a loving husband, David, who has supported me from the beginning with my first psychotic break happening on our honeymoon. Not many husbands would stick around after that took place. We have three beautiful girls who are healthy. When people think of a disorder like schizoaffective disorder, they do not think that if you have it you can function and lead a normal life, but you can. Schizoaffective disorder is described as a mental disorder that can cause loss of touch with reality, psychosis or mood problems. The disorder has cycles of severe symptoms, such as paranoid thoughts, delusions, hallucinations, mood problems, trouble sleeping, poor hygiene and trouble concentrating. Between cycles of severe symptoms are cycles where the patient appears normal with no problems. My cycles of severe symptoms were few compared with the cycles where I was fine.

I started having mental illness problems on my honeymoon in October of 1997. Up until then I had no problems with mental illness. I had completed college with a degree in computer science and was in the marching band. Handling school and being active in the marching band involved a lot of stress and I seemed to handle that pressure well. After I got out of school, got an apartment and started my job in the real world, I started to notice some mood problems. When situations did not go my way, I would get upset very easily. It was like I could not control my emotions, especially around my time of the month. I really did not think anything of this and just chalked it up to having awful PMS disorder. It may even have been PMDD or premenstrual dysphoric disorder, which is a more severe form of PMS. The symptoms of PMDD are feeling more depressed than usual, anxiety, mood swings, crying easily, feeling tired, having trouble sleeping and other physical symptoms.

One

The Wedding

David and I had met in college. We dated on and off for three years in college. At the end of college David proposed to me and I said yes. We were very happy and were looking forward to spending our lives together.

Leading up to our wedding, I wanted to make everything just right. You wait for that special day to happen, and you just want it to be exactly how you pictured it without any mistakes. I was working really hard on the details of the wedding. I wanted everything to be perfect. The day before the wedding I had started my period, so I was feeling a little out of sorts. The rehearsal at the church and dinner went nicely. Everyone had a good time and I was really looking forward to getting married. After dinner we went over to the reception hall to prepare it for the next day. Everything was going well. I seemed to be doing fine. When I got home to my mom's house and tried to fall asleep, I just could not. I was just too excited about the big day. I was anxious and just wanted everything to go according to plan. I definitely knew David was the man for me and I deeply loved him. I just wanted our day to reflect that.

The morning came, and although I did not get any sleep, I felt fine. The photographer came over and took plenty of photographs.

Before long it was time to take the limousine to the church. We got to the church rather early, and it seemed like forever before it was time for the wedding to start. At 1:00 the wedding started. I was anxious and nervous to get married. The flowers were just lovely and the bridesmaids wore flowing maroon gowns. My dress was a beautiful full white gown with lace sleeves. The wedding was exactly how I always pictured it to be.

After the wedding, the wedding party went to a garden to get photographs taken with the beautiful fall foliage. Once we got to the reception hall, people were hungry because we had been gone so long. We ate as soon as we arrived there, and the food was wonderful. David and I were having a great time talking to family and friends. David was busting a move on the dance floor, and he was a treat to watch. I really felt like I was so lucky to have a guy like him, and I could not have been happier.

At the end of the night, my brother Rob drove us to a hotel near the Pittsburgh airport. We were leaving for Cancun, Mexico, in the morning. Once we got to the room, I could not relax again. Once again I could not sleep. I was starting to panic that I was not able to fall asleep. So now I was going on two days without any rest and I think it was starting to catch up with me.

The next morning we took a taxi to the airport where we boarded a plane to Cancun. After we landed, we caught a taxi to Tulum, which is where our hotel was. Once we got there and took a look at our hotel, I insisted we get transferred to Cancun. The hotel was dirty, and there was no running hot water. We finally got moved to a hotel in Cancun. Two women entered the room beside us and David said maybe they were lesbians. Soon after checking in, we were in for the night and I started to become paranoid. I thought the hotel staff was listening to our conversations and that there were cameras in the room. I could not relax. I even tried to take a bath. Nothing seemed to help. Once again I could not fall asleep. Many thoughts were jumbled in my mind. I felt like my brain was melting. The more I tried to sleep, the worse my thoughts were.

Then sometime in the morning I felt a pop in my head. I thought I had a bleed in my brain. My head ached and I felt very strange. I remember waking up the next morning and not being myself. I was hallucinating and thought my husband was the devil. I kept saying I was a lesbian. I thought I was dead. David checked us out of the hotel and all he wanted was to get me home. He had no idea what was going on, and neither did I. Once we got to the airport and boarded the plane, I was making a scene. Airport security had to escort us off the airplane. I was still having hallucinations and thinking that David was evil. We then took a cab to the Cancun hospital. The world appeared differently to me. While in the cab, I kept thinking it was slowing down and stopping and then starting again. It was a very scary experience. I remember reading signs along the road and thinking that they were saying evil things. I really thought I was in hell, and it was a horrible experience.

Once I got to the hospital, the staff heavily sedated me with Haldol. I felt blackness come over me. I was out for days. I remember waking up and feeling very drugged and not knowing what had happened to me. I asked David if I had died or been near death because that is what I felt like the whole experience was. I was completely blacked out for days. I do not remember anything. David was sleeping on the couch in my room, and he looked shocked and confused. He probably had no idea what had happened and had been through his own hell. I felt terrible that I had put him through this. This is not what I had pictured our honeymoon to be. I wanted romantic walks on the beach, but we never even got to see the water. My mother and father-in-law decided to fly down to Cancun to help get us out of the hospital and back home. Once they arrived, I think David was relieved that he did not have to get me home on his own. When they got there, I was still very drugged. I could not stand without falling over and was very drowsy. They had to put me in a wheelchair in the airport because I could not walk. I was quiet on the flight home. I did not know how to act or what to say.

When we got home, I went to see my family doctor and he recommended that I see a psychiatrist. The psychiatrist did not think I needed to be put on medicine since this was the first time that it happened. He thought my symptoms were merely the result of the stress I experienced in planning for the wedding. He wanted me to get a CT-scan to rule out MS or other neurological problems. The scan came back normal, which was a relief. Everyone in my family just thought at the time that this was a one-time occurrence and would not happen again.

After the honeymoon, everything went back to normal. I told everyone at work that I drank the water in Cancun and had gotten sick and that I was fine now. I just proceeded to go on with my life like nothing had happened.

Two

Second Hospitalization

Everything went back to normal, and I was fine without any problems until about May of 1998, when I went on a training seminar for work in Stamford, Connecticut. It was a week-long session about how the business worked. I met some people and was talking, and we decided we were going to play a game of Pictionary. This was my first mistake because I do not have one artistic bone in my body. I attempted to draw and they started to laugh at my drawings. I started to feel very self-conscious, as if people were talking about me behind my back. The next morning at breakfast, I swore I could hear whispers about me. That evening a group of us decided to go into New York. I could not relax and enjoy the sights. I had trouble falling asleep that night, and in the morning, I started hallucinating. I refused to leave my room. I did not want to embarrass myself in front of my peers. I eventually ended up talking to someone and that person went ahead and called an ambulance. I could not believe this was happening again, and at the worse time possible.

The company was nice enough to allow my husband fly out on the company jet. I only stayed in the hospital a couple of days. I recovered quickly on the medicine given to me in the hospital. When I returned home, I went to see my psychiatrist and he felt he had no choice but to put me on medicine. He chose Risperdal, an antipsychotic medication. I did not understand why this kept happening to me. No one in my family suffered from mental illness. I did not fit the stereotype of someone with a mental illness. I just did not want to admit that I had such a condition. I decided to take my medicine. I just did not want to end up in the hospital again. I did not want to keep hurting David. I wanted more than anything to lead a normal life. It just seemed that, whenever I was put under a lot of stress, it would trigger this illness in my brain.

Three

The Pregnancy

Two years passed with no problems. The medicine was working well. Then, in April of 2000, I became pregnant with my first child. The pregnancy was unplanned. I was happy, but in the back of my mind I did not know if I was ready to have children. After talking with my psychiatrist, he agreed that I could go off the medicine completely since I had been doing so well the past two years. I had no problems until I was about 5 months pregnant. In September of 2000, I started having problems sleeping. It got so bad that I had to go to the emergency room, and Katie, my baby, was in distress and needed fluids. I could have lost Katie, which would have been horrible. I was admitted to the psychiatric section of the hospital. I remember waking up in the middle of the night with a terrible dream that I had lost my baby, and I got up out of bed and walked down the hall. I remember someone that worked there walked me back to my room and comforted me. While I was in the hospital, they put me on Haldol, which back then was one of the drugs believed to be safe to take during pregnancy. I remember about every hour of the night, they would come in and check on the baby to make sure she had a heart beat. I just kept praying that we would make it out of there okay.

After I left the hospital, I was not the same person as I had been. The Haldol made me a changed person. It was almost like my eyes were open and I was functioning, but I was not home. I was very tired all the time, and I felt like my brain was in left field. The rest of the pregnancy went as well as could be expected. I passed my due date and eventually was induced on February 1, 2001. On the next day, I experienced some contractions but never really dilated past a one. So around 3:30 p.m., the doctors decided to do a C-section. I remember being extremely scared that everything was happening so fast. The surgery went well and Katie was born around 4:20 p.m., a healthy 7 pounds, 8 ounces. I remember she came out exceptionally hungry and I could not breastfeed her because I was on Haldol. I was not extremely bonded to Katie. I felt at the time I was not ready to have children and thus did not feel a bond to her immediately.

When I came home, my mom stayed with me for a while. I did a lot of lying on the couch and sleeping. I decided I did not want to go back to work full-time and that I wanted to see if I could work three days a week instead. I stayed on Haldol and was very tired all the time. Haldol was probably one of the worst drugs I was on. It made me drool and continually made me feel very tired. I really did not feel like doing anything when I was on it. I felt like I was missing out on being a mother. I was not able to experience motherhood the way I wanted to because of the medicine.

Four

My World is Coming to an End

I was fine for probably about six or seven months, and then I had another episode in the beginning of September 2001. I thought that the world was coming to an end and that I was in hell. I thought I was dead and the ambulance had to come to take me to the hospital. I kept saying that the world was coming to an end. Shortly after I got out of the hospital, my husband was in a head-on collision. While he was driving to work, his car hydroplaned across the median and hit a car head on. Miraculously, he survived with only bad whiplash and back pain, for which he had to see a physical therapist. I remember wondering if anything else bad could happen to us.

Shortly after I got out of the hospital, I was scheduled to get a colonoscopy. I had been diagnosed with ulcerative colitis when I was fourteen and had to get regular checkups to check for precancerous cells. I went in for the procedure on September 11, 2001, and my colon was not cleaned out well enough for the doctor to do the procedure. When they pulled me out of the procedure room, the television screens were showing the planes hitting the towers in New York. I started to think maybe the world really was coming to an end with this attack. The reality of what was happening in the world did not help my condition.

The next few weeks were rough. I ended up in the hospital again in the beginning of October, but this time it was different. I had a new doctor, Dr. Baylor, and he had put me on Thorazine and blood pressure medicine. He had me on a high dose of blood pressure medicine for some reason and many times I thought I was going to pass out because of it.

When I was admitted to the hospital, the doctors and nurses thought that I had overdosed. Prior to arriving at the hospital, I had taken approximately 1000 mg of Thorazine. Dr. Baylor had told me it would be okay to take that much. After I was admitted, I was afraid to close my eyes. I was deeply afraid that I might never wake. I just laid there with a sheet pulled up to my neck as doctors and nurses came in to check on me every few minutes. I was terrified. I waited there with my mom and husband many hours before the insurance company gave permission for me to be admitted. I clearly should have overdosed, but I think God kept me alive for some reason.

Once I was in the hospital, my mom and husband still came to visit me, but the time in the hospital was dragging. Each day seemed like an eternity. Also, in the bathroom's shower the hot side was cold and the cold side was hot. There was also this very scary male nurse with long painted black fingernails. I remember reading a book and he said he did not think I could understand a book. These minor details may have not bothered most people, but they can really affect someone with a mental illness. In addition, the television shows and movies seemed different and scarier. This is not the first time television appeared differently to me. The night before I left, it was like I was having a dream where everything was moving fast in front of me. The trees and wind and sun and many days were passing, and then I woke up. When I woke up, I saw that my name band was gone. Most people would say that it probably just fell off. This really bothered me because I could not find it anywhere. I looked under the bed and everywhere but it had just disappeared. My mom and my husband came to get me and told me just to forget about it and get my stuff so we could get out of there.

When I got home from the hospital I felt extremely sick and I was throwing up. I also felt more tired than usual. I made an appointment to see the doctor. The doctor did some tests and then called me and had me come into his office. He told me that the way the blood work looked indicated that I could have leukemia. He said he was going to contact another doctor and see if the test results might be indicative of flu or something less serious. The other doctor said it was possible, so I just had to come back in a couple of weeks to have another blood test. When I had the second blood test, it came back normal. My husband and I then decided Dr. Baylor did not have my best interests at heart, so I made a switch to a new doctor, Dr. Tamen.

When I first met Dr. Tamen, he told me that I did not fit the mold of a schizophrenic. I totally agreed with him because I never really thought I had schizophrenia or schizoaffective disorder. More than anything else in the world, all I ever wanted was to be happy and to not struggle with this illness anymore. I saw Dr. Tamen along with a therapist, and everything was going well for many months. I was on a good medicine now called Seroquel, which was a newer antipsychotic that had fewer side effects than the older drugs, like Thorazine. I was happy and enjoying being a mother to Katie. Things were starting to look up.

Five

Move to Indianapolis

In June of 2002, my husband decided to take a job in Indianapolis, Indiana, and we prepared to make the move from Cincinnati. David's brother lived in Brownsburg, which was about 30 miles from Carmel, where we were looking to move. Also, David's parents lived in Fort Wayne, Indiana, which would also be closer. We decided mainly to move to be closer to family, so if we needed help in the future they would be more accessible. We decided to move into an apartment while we built a house. We lived in the apartment from June of 2002 until after Christmas that year.

During our stay in the apartment, my daughter Katie turned 18 months old, and we were concerned that she did not have that many words in her vocabulary. Her pediatrician recommended that we get her evaluated by First Steps. After the evaluation, we found out that she qualified for services through First Steps and that it appeared that she might have autism. The news was devastating to us. Thoughts ran through my head about whether I had caused her autism from being in the hospital and being put on Haldol. There was no one to tell me that there was a one hundred percent chance that the Haldol did not cause her autism. I had to carry around this guilt that my illness may have harmed the health of one of my children. To deal with this possible diagnosis of autism, David and I hit early intervention hard. Not only did she have First Steps, but we put her in private speech therapy also.

Around the first of January, we moved into our new house. Katie was making great strides in her therapies through First Steps. David and I were happy with the progress she was making, but knew she would probably continue speech therapy until she started first grade.

I was doing well until Labor Day weekend of 2003. I thought I was pregnant, so I went off my medicine and started to have problems. I always wanted to have two children, a boy and a girl, and when I thought I might be pregnant, I did not tell anyone and went off my medicine. I started having problems sleeping and began to hear noises that were not there. It was like my hearing sense was amplified and I could hear a pin drop all the way downstairs, or so I thought. One thing different about my illness as compared with other people with schizoaffective disorder is that I never really heard any voices telling me to do anything. However, a lot of times I would hear a song on the radio and think the song was about me, and how I should let my husband go. Television shows would also appear more graphic and scarier to me when I was having an episode.

My husband proceeded to take me to the emergency room. The staff prescribed some medicine to help me sleep, but it did not work. I had started my menstrual cycle; which many of my hospitalizations happened around that time of the month for some reason. Finally, since I was not getting any better, my husband decided to take me to St. Thomas More Stress Center. As we were driving there, I remember the rain was coming down so hard that cars were off the side of the road. The day I was admitted to the hospital, September 1, 2003, Indianapolis received the most rain ever in one calendar day — 7.2 inches. I almost felt as though God was upset with me and was telling me through rain. I now know this was just a coincidence that we received all this rain on that day.

We entered the hospital and had to wait a long time before I was admitted. They had to call my insurance for pre-authorization, which took many hours. I remember a man walked down the stairs and said "she is going to have a heart attack." I started to panic and asked David if he heard him say that, and he answered no. My heart began to race and I thought I was going to die right there of a heart attack. I was hearing people saying things that other people were not hearing, and it was very frightening and real to me. I kept wondering how an illness could really affect your brain like this. Once I was admitted, I had no idea that this would be one of the two worst mental hospital stays of my life.

When I was taken up to the ward, I had to answer a series of questions. I was then shown to my room. I remember the first night I hardly slept at all. I wanted to keep the bathroom door open with the light on, but it kept closing all the way. I finally put a garbage can in the doorway to keep it from closing. My roommate was not very friendly. For example, one day when I woke up, she had put a list of the seven deadly sins on my nightstand. The whole Labor Day weekend, TBS was showing the movie "Seven" over and over again. When I tried to watch the movie there in the hospital, it was like I was watching a completely different version of the movie. It was much more violent and contained scenes and dialogue that were not in the original movie.

When I was a patient, it seemed to me that some of the staff was actually trying to make me worse. When the nurses would check my vitals, they would pretend like the machine was not working and my vitals were zero. I kept checking my pulse to see if my heart was still beating. My psychiatrist in the hospital was giving me high doses of a medicine that was making my heart race, and I really thought I was going to have a heart attack in there. I complained about it to my husband and he got the psychiatrist to taper the medicine down, but it is very scary when you trust the doctors and it seems like they do not have your best interest at heart. There was a patient that was forcing me to read Job in the Bible. Was she trying to tell me that I was going to end up like Job, with nothing? I did not want to read the Bible, and she was upsetting me. There was also an older gentleman who could tell the past or future of other patients, at least that is what it seemed. He kept trying to tell me that I had died before.

I got to the point where I could no longer take being in the hospital. So one day after my family left from visiting, I sat by the door, and when the last person left, I stuck my foot in the door. I quietly snuck out the door and down the stairs and then waved good-bye to the person at the hospital front desk and left. I ran across the parking lot and crossed the street, and I eventually got to a drug store where I called my sister-in-law to come to get me. She came and drove me back to my house. I begged my family not to take me back there. I told them it was a type of hell and that I did not want to go back. My family explained to me that I had to go back to the hospital.

Once I returned back to the hospital, I had to wear pajamas for a week. I started to become paranoid that everyone was against me. I kept thinking that the doctors and nurses wanted to keep me there forever. The longer I was in the hospital; it became increasingly harder to urinate. I would drink and drink but it was so hard to urinate. I remember wondering if my body was just shutting down. People would be admitted all the time. I remember this girl saying she had been in a car accident and she did not understand why she was there. Another lady said she remembered being rushed to the hospital and that she just woke up there. She hoped that her husband would be back for her, but she did not know for sure. I kept thinking,

Lora Bell

"Where am I?" I remember patients in the eating area were dancing to the music of the jukebox, but in fact it was pulled away from the wall and not even plugged in. How could this be happening?

After about two weeks in the hospital, I was finally released to go home. I was so thankful that I was out of there. I said to David, "Promise me that you will never take me back to St Thomas More Stress Center again." He replied, "You will never have to go back there. I promise."

This hospital visit really affected David. I think he thought when we moved to Indianapolis we would have a fresh start and that there would be no more hospital stays. I really felt like I let my family down by going off my medicine and I promised David that I would never come off my medicine again without the doctor's permission. David said to me, "Lora if you go off your medicine again, we are through." I said to David, "I promise you I will not."

Six

Another Baby?

The next year and a half went really well. I was not having any problems, but I really wanted to have another baby. More than anything else I wanted Katie to have a brother or sister. My husband was content with one, and with all the problems I had experienced, he did not want to risk me having any more. I wrote him a letter about how much it meant to me to have another child, and in October of 2005, he said, "yes." We conceived that month and I was extremely happy.

Early in the pregnancy I had what they called a "bleed," where there is a separation in the uterine wall. The bleed eventually corrected itself with shots of progesterone and with me being careful of how much weight I carried. I had no problems whatsoever with my mental illness throughout the pregnancy. I was doing very well with the stress of being pregnant and being a mom to Katie. I thought that I was going to have a boy, but we found out in February that the baby was in fact another girl. I think David was a little disappointed. He always wanted a boy, someone to play baseball and watch "Star Wars" movies with.

On June 15, 2006, I went in to have my C-section, and Rose Ann was born. She was a healthy 6 pounds, 11 ounces. While the doctor was performing the C-section, he noticed that my appendix did not look good. He decided to go ahead and take it out, which made the operation a little longer. Because I had my appendix out, I had to stay in the hospital an extra day to recuperate. I really wanted to get home, but the doctor wanted me to stay.

Once I got home, it took me some time to get around without being in a lot of pain, but overall things were going well. My mom came up to visit and stayed a week to help out. After my mom went home, all of a sudden I started to have problems. It started with muscle spasms. I would be laying still and my muscles would start to twitch. I would start thinking that I was not going to be around to see my kids grow up and that I was going to get some horrible illness. These thoughts started to overwhelm me. My physical symptoms started to become worse. I was experiencing muscle pain and weakness. My eyesight was getting worse, or at least I thought it was. I was trying to diagnose myself on the Internet. I had numbness in my fingers and toes. I thought I had MS or ALS. The brain is such a powerful organ that if you think you have something seriously wrong with you then your body acts like you do. I was having trouble urinating, which reminded me of when I was in the hospital in 2003 and I was having similar issues and thinking my body was shutting down. I had to call my mom for her to come back up, which made me feel terrible. I could not get out of my mind that I had a serious illness.

Once my mom arrived I acted like a complete child. I could not sleep and would cry and carry on in front of her. I could not make the symptoms stop and kept focusing on them, which only made them worse in my head. I know that I made the symptoms worse in my head, but I was really experiencing muscle spasms and pain. These symptoms were very real and serious to me. My mom felt like I was doing all of this for attention. I was not. My whole family thought I was making my symptoms up. At this time I had no idea that postpartum depression could manifest with physical symptoms. My mom took me to the doctor's office and got them to agree to do a MRI to put my mind at ease. The results came back and were normal. I was ecstatic. I was up one moment and then down the next. However, my symptoms did not go immediately away. I was put on Zoloft, which is an antidepressant and experienced a period of time where I could not eat. I desperately wanted to eat, but I felt no hunger. My psychiatrist believed that what I was experiencing was related to postpartum depression. I was very close to being admitted to the hospital again and I am so thankful that my family helped keep me out. I truly do not know if I would have gotten out of the hospital if I had been admitted.

This difficult time was also taking its toll on Katie. She could sense there was something wrong with me and there was nothing I could do about it. I had anxiety attacks so badly that I could not sleep or relax. I thought I was going to die and I was scared because I thought that if I did die I was going to hell. I always had a fear of dying since I was little. I guess it is the unknown that scares me the most. I always believed in God, but nobody is ever sure they are going to go to heaven. I feared that my hell was going to be the stress center at St. Thomas More hospital and that I would never get out of there. I would spend all eternity there alone with no family and loved ones. I guess these fears have made me be stronger and not give up. There have been many times I have felt like the mental hospital was hell, but I refused to believe it. I just prayed and hoped for the best.

After a few weeks I started to do better and my mom returned home to Pennsylvania. I am just so thankful that I did not have to go back to the stress center. I really did not know if I could have handled that experience. I do not think I have ever had a good experience at a mental health facility, expect maybe in Stamford, Connecticut. I think that is the only time I was treated well. Maybe in the back of my mind I was not convinced I was practicing the right religion, or doing the right things with my life.

Seven

Religion Problems

My husband and I got married in the Catholic church. I grew up Catholic and my husband attended a Presbyterian church. One of the requirements for getting married in a Catholic church is to promise to raise your children as Catholics. We both made that promise prior to getting married. At the beginning of our marriage in Cincinnati, we were not really members of a Catholic church so we did not go to church regularly. Once we moved to Indianapolis, we became members at a Catholic church close to our house. We both attended most Sundays, but we still were not making church a priority. Once Katie turned the age where she started to go to Sunday school, we were really trying to make the effort. Then, shortly after Rose was born, my husband had a dream in which God came to him and said that he was disappointed in how David was living his life. He did not tell me about the dream at the time. He just started to read the Bible. He was soon reading and studying the Bible every night and taking notes. What was I doing while he was doing this? Nothing. I took no interest in the Bible even though I had recovered from some horrible experiences in the hospital and should have wanted to become more knowledgeable about the Bible. After reading the Bible for many months, David had another dream in which he saw an angel showing him around the heavens. The angel told David that this could be all his if he just took the next step. Soon after that dream, David decided to get baptized at a non-denominational Church of Christ. In the following months, he began to attend this non-denominational Church of Christ. I continued to go to the Catholic Church and take Katie to her Sunday school classes while David attended his own church. This was very difficult on our family, but I felt like I was choosing the right religion at the time.

Everything was going well with Rose and Katie. Katie started kindergarten in August of 2006, and she was doing well. Katie had progressed very well with her speech at this point and if someone did not know Katie they would have never guessed she had autism. Rose was a really good baby, and I was very happy and content with my two girls. Then when Rose was about 10 months old I found out that I was pregnant with my third. It was unexpected and quite a surprise, but I was excited to be having another baby. At that time I was on some anti-anxiety medicine that I had to discontinue. Anxiety medicine can cause birth defects so it was really important to taper off of it quickly. It was harder than I thought to get off the anxiety medicine. I had to go down to a half a pill at first for a few days and then off of it all together. I had a little trouble the first few nights falling asleep. I was relieved, though, when I was off the medicine completely. I did not want to become dependent on it.

When I had my first ultrasound at six weeks, I once again had a bleed inside like I had with Rose, but it was much worse this time. I had to get ultrasounds every couple of weeks to monitor the bleed. I also had to get shots of progesterone, which has been proven to help heal a bleed. We were scared we were going to lose the baby. David prayed a lot and I prayed too. Then, at about 14 weeks, the doctor said there was still a bleed there but it was almost healed. We were relieved. All of our prayers had been answered. I knew that David deeply wanted a boy so I knew when we went for the 18-week ultrasound he was hoping for the news of a boy. Sara, the ultrasound technician, checked and reported that we were going to have another girl. I was happy I was having another girl. I would have loved to have given David a boy, but it was just not meant to be. David and I were meant to raise three beautiful girls and we are so lucky to have them.

The rest of the pregnancy went really well. David continued going to the Church of Christ while I attended my Catholic church. Sometimes I would go with David to his church. During this time, it was very hard on the family because we were not always attending church together. David and I were split on a major topic in our relationship and it was tough to repair. I took the oath seriously to raise our children as Catholics and I felt that he had just kind of brushed it off.

On January 18, 2008, I went into the hospital to have my baby. The C-section went well and Shelly Marie was born a healthy 6 pounds, 12 ounces. She had a full head of dark hair and I noticed that her nose was wider than the other two girls, but she was perfect in my eyes.

My mother-in-law stayed and helped me the first week back from the hospital. During that first week, David came home from work early one day with some bad news. He had been laid off from his job. This was devastating news to come just one week after we had a baby. He only had three weeks of severance and no health insurance. I broke down and started to cry. I cried to David, "What are we going to do?" He responded, "We are going to be okay. I have a couple weeks severance." David put together his resume and began searching for a job right away. He distributed his resume to his church and got great responses. I should have seen how supportive the church was at that time, but I did not. In the meantime, the church had arranged to deliver us meals for two weeks while I recuperated from the C-section, which was very nice. The church was really like a family.

   Soon after David sent out the email, a lady at church got him an interview at a growing company in Carmel. The interview went well and he was offered a job. We were ecstatic, but he had some doubts whether he could handle the job. He decided to take the job but he soon found out that it was going to be a rough road ahead. This job was going to take much more dedication than his previous job. He had to work nights and most weekends and it was hard on the family in the beginning. It was especially hard on me because I was doing the nightly feedings and taking care of the baby most nights while he worked. Everything was going well with me. I wasn't having any serious problems. I was, however, having some minor problems with my memory. I would find myself forgetting things and rechecking over and over to make certain I had everything before I left the house. But overall I was doing well. I was handling the stresses of life pretty well.

Eight

Christmas in Indianapolis

Around October we decided that the family was going to celebrate Christmas in Indianapolis this year. My mother- and father-in-law live in Fort Wayne and we usually travel up there and spend two nights to celebrate Christmas. This year we decided that we were going to host Christmas in Indianapolis. My mother- and father-in-law would spend a night at each of their son's houses. The first night would be Christmas night at our house and then the next morning we would go to my brother- and sister-in-law's house and have breakfast. After breakfast we would open gifts. The problems for me started a couple of days before Christmas. I started to think I was pregnant again. I had my tubes tied after my third daughter was born in January of 2008, but I was reading on the Internet that it was possible to still get pregnant. Since I got pregnant so easily with all my children, I thought maybe it was a possibility. I told my husband that my body did not seem like my period was going to start. So he went out and bought a pregnancy test. It was negative, which was a relief because I was having a hard time managing my three daughters who were then eight, two and a half and almost one.

Christmas Eve started out well. I had been getting good sleep up until then and felt like we were going to have a nice Christmas. That night we decided to meet my brother- and sister-in-law for dinner and then go to church with them at a Church of Christ on their side of town. On the way to the restaurant, Rose, my two and a half year old, fell asleep. When we got to the restaurant, she woke up very cranky and would not calm down. She made numerous scenes and I was starting to get stares from other people. We finally got her to calm down somewhat and we had dinner. I had to hold her on my lap the whole time and really could not eat. Towards the end of dinner, I finally had to take her out to the car. We decided that since Rose was behaving so badly we would just go home and not go to church. The whole restaurant ordeal did not stress me out at all. I have had to deal with situations like that in restaurants before. However, I was kind of upset that I was not able to go to a church of some kind on Christmas Eve. In the past, I had always made an effort to go to church on Christmas Eve.

We got home and finally got the kids to go to bed. David and I then worked to get Christmas set up in our basement for our kids. We got all the presents out and finished wrapping some last-minute gifts. I do not think we went to bed until well after midnight. We both were extremely exhausted. Once again I slept very well.

On Christmas morning, the kids got up and they opened their stockings. Everything seemed to be going okay but I was finding myself not being able to really enjoy Christmas like I should have been. We had gone way overboard for my oldest daughter Katie. She got everything she wanted and then some. I started to feel sick to my stomach that she was going to think that she was always going to get whatever she wanted. She wanted an old Nintendo 64 and my husband found one and surprised her with it. She did not need this and she would have been able to understand if she did not get it. I then started to worry about everything that needed to get done before company arrived. I was on a mission to make everything as perfect as possible. I started to make my dishes for the dinner and cleaned up the house. Katie kept asking over and over again when her cousins were going to get here. It was starting to drain me. In the meantime, I had started my period on Christmas Day, of all days.

Around 3:00, my brother- and sister-in-law's family arrived. My father- and mother-in-law got into town around 4:30. David was going through a lot of trouble to make chicken wings in his turkey fryer. He kept obsessively wiping down counters and sweeping the floor as he was cooking; which was starting to make me nervous. Around 5:30, it was time to eat. The food was perfect. Carrie, my sister-in-law, helped me make stuffed mushrooms, which were delicious. Everyone loved the food, but I noticed myself not paying attention to what people were saying. It was like my mind was somewhere else. I was eating my dinner and got up and went to get some more mushrooms. I noticed that there were several left. So I took two more. Then, while I was eating them, I came to the realization that there were not several left, but instead, there were only two and I had taken the last two. I started to think I was selfish and that I never thought of anyone else but myself. The rest of the night I really could not let myself enjoy the company of the others. I felt like I could not say anything right and that I was a phony.

John and Sue, my mother- and father-in-law, retired to the basement and my sister- and brother-in-law left for the night. David and I then straightened up the kitchen, after which we put the kids to sleep.

When I went to bed that night, thoughts of being selfish filled my head. I thought back to the mushrooms and wondered how my mind could have seen many mushrooms when in fact there were only two. Gosh, I must really be crazy. I was thinking that I got pregnant because I liked the attention and that I was narcissistic. For months prior to Christmas, I was glued to the television watching

Nancy Grace every night at 8:00 p.m. talk about the Caylee Anthony case. I was obsessed with it. She was being labeled as narcissistic, so I began to think that I was a little like her. Maybe I only cared about myself and I got pregnant to get attention from my family. I also gambled a lot and had recently gone to a casino by myself and lost lots of money. I thought maybe I did this to get attention or maybe to show that I could do it. I started to have terrible thoughts about whether I would cry if I lost someone close to me. How would I react? When I was eleven I lost my dad to cancer, and I do not think I ever really cried about it. Why do I not remember much about my dad? I know that he worked a lot as a bricklayer and that I spent most of my time taking dancing lessons. I remember before he died he apologized to me for not getting to spend much time with me. I had trouble letting go of these thoughts and, as a result, I did not sleep that well.

David woke me up the next morning. I felt rushed and hurried to get everything together. We had to be over at my brother- and sister-in-law's at 10:00 for breakfast. Once we arrived there I had a hard time relaxing. The whole time I was there I kept trying to do things for others. I would get people drinks or food, anything to not label me as selfish. I remember my husband made a comment about Luke and Carrie, my brother- and sister-in-law, possibly having another baby. Then he also said that he felt sad that he would never have a boy. I knew deep down he always wanted to have a boy, but it just was not meant to be. We had three girls and that is what God wanted us to have. After breakfast we opened presents, and again, all the comments I made seemed to me to be bogus. It was like I had nothing genuine to say.

After we opened presents, my mother-in-law, sister-in-law and I decided to go shopping. We went up to Zionsville to an upscale kids' store named Jack and Jill. On our way up to the store, the roads were covered with thick fog. It was kind of a creepy night. I remember we had a conversation about whether I or my sister-in-law Carrie would ever be willing to move to another city. I said that I really liked the area here and would not want to learn a new town. I remember Carrie responded that she would not dismiss moving for her own personal reasons. I took that as another selfish thought of mine. When we got to the store, I thought everything was just too expensive. I told Sue that Shelly, my one-year-old, did not need anything. But it seemed like I could not say anything right. After that store, we went to Target and I broke down to Sue, and said, "I am a selfish person and I just think of myself." Sue told me to talk to Carrie. I confided in Carrie and said, "I feel like a phony and the words coming out of my mouth are not genuine." I pulled myself together then, but when we got back to Carrie's house I could not function. I could not find my shoes. I did not know where to look for my purse. We finally got all our stuff together, loaded up the car and started on our way home. I broke down and started crying to my husband David. He comforted me and said, "Lora, this has been a stressful time and now it is over." I told him how I thought I was selfish and that I did things to get attention. I told David, "I gambled and lost money for attention and I got pregnant for attention." I know he was hurt and was upset that this was happening again. I know deep down he feared that this could be the beginning of an episode where I could end up in the hospital.

Nine

My Condition Gets Worse

On Saturday December 27, I do not remember much except that David's mom and dad stopped by before going home to Fort Wayne. I could tell that they sensed something was wrong. In fact, my condition got worse because of their visit. For example, everything out of their mouths was negative — the economy is in turmoil, there are no jobs out there, everything is falling apart about the world. When they left, I felt even more depressed. After they were gone, I tried to make a grocery list to pick up a few things for dinners. I decided to go to Marsh, which was right across the street. The trip to the store did not go well for me. I remember I went to the deli to get some Lorriane swiss cheese. The guy behind the counter was acting very frustrated because he could not find the cheese. I finally told him I would just take the Lacy swiss cheese. It rang up as Lorriane swiss cheese and was in fact Lorriane cheese. The worker's behavior did not help my condition. Then, as I was shopping, I kept hearing on the speaker for Lora to call this number. It was though my senses were heightened and that small things that went wrong were magnified a hundred percent. I also did not recognize one single worker there and I shop at Marsh all the time. As I came home to my husband, I was crying for him to please not to send me to hell. I was talking about the St. Thomas More Stress Center, which to me was like a hell on earth.

On Sunday, David called his mom to come down and help. Luckily she did not have to go to work that week. I remember I started to wake up with sweats. I wondered why I was waking up in sweats. Thoughts that I could be in hell started to enter my mind. We sent Katie, my oldest, to stay two nights at her cousin's house. I did not want her to see me in this condition. Carrie came over to pick up Katie, and I told her David had told me to take three Geodon, but really he had told me to take two. Geodon was a newer antipsychotic medicine. I knew at this point that no amount of medicine was going to help me. She went upstairs and came back down and reassured me that I had not overdosed. I remember Carrie talking about Christmas and how she was disappointed that she did not get an Ulta gift card. I was very careful not to criticize my Christmas gifts because I did not want to seem materialistic or selfish.

Sunday night did not go well. I wanted to go to church with David that night but he refused to take me because he could not have me doing anything that I would regret. That night, as I was feeding Shelly, I was listening to a news channel on the television. Someone came on and said that they were having really bad anxiety and stress and wondered if there even was a God. This really upset me because I was suffering from severe anxiety and stress, but I knew God existed. I believe in God and that for some reason I needed to go through this test and come out on the other end a stronger Christian than before. This was happening to me as a wake-up call that I need to start living my life better.

When I woke up on Monday in sweats, I ran downstairs. I could not function. I was wondering why David was not working when he has such a demanding job. I noticed that Rose seemed scared of me and did not want to be around me. Shelly was spitting up and she had not spit up for a few months. I was very indecisive and began to question whether I was dead or not. I could not eat and it seemed like everyone else was not eating or drinking. I thought I was dead and was questioning how long I had been dead and if I had even had Shelly or Rose. The days seemed like they were flying and I was not getting anything done.

Monday night I slept pretty well but I again woke up with sweats. I told David I thought I should go to the hospital. He told me I should take a shower before I go because he knew how I liked to be clean. I went ahead and took a shower. After my shower, Walgreen's Pharmacy called and needed my license number to fill my anxiety medicine. I told Walgreen's that I would drive over and give it to them. I wanted to get out of the house and judge how things appeared. David hesitated before agreeing to take me, but he refused to let me go into Walgreen's. I knew I was not getting any better, but I knew that if I went into the hospital, it would be hell on earth to me and that I might never ever get out.

When we got back from Walgreen's, my mom called to talk to me. I asked, "Mom, is this really happening?" She answered, "Yes." Then she questioned, "Why is Shelly's hair so blond?" My mom wondered why Shelly was the only one of my children with blue eyes and blond hair. The other two had darker eyes and dark hair, like David and me. Then it was almost as if I heard God speaking through her. Later, I came to the conclusion that it was Satan that I was hearing. She said, "I heard your prayers. You asked to be a better mother, daughter, daughter-in-law, sister, sister-in-law and aunt every Sunday." I ran from the phone. How did she know my prayers? I would learn later after I got out of the hospital that these prayers were vain and repetitive. Every Sunday at my Catholic church, I would pray to God to help me be a better mother, daughter, daughter-in-law, wife, and so on. I do not know why I prayed for this. I think I was suffering from low self-esteem. I am a good mother and I was back then too. Soon after I joined the Church of Christ, one of the first things I learned in Bible study was about vain and repetitive prayers. Was this just a coincidence? After my conversation with my mother, we were deciding whether to go to Carmel St. Thomas More Hospital or not. Sue, David's mom, could not make up her mind either. She said, "Well, maybe she would get better here, but on the other hand, I think she needs to go to the hospital." She kept going back and forth between the two. What was making her be like this? Finally, we packed up my things and left for the hospital.

Ten

Hospital Stay

We were supposed to go to St. Thomas More Carmel Hospital, not St. Thomas More Stress Center in Indianapolis. While we were driving, Dr. King's office called to say not to take me to St. Thomas More Carmel Hospital, but instead, to take me to the Indianapolis St. Thomas More Stress Center. We came to find out there is not even a stress center in Carmel. Why then were they going to send me there? My worst fears were becoming realized. When David hung up, he said, "It is done." I thought, does this mean that finally I am being put away forever? As we were driving, I asked David, "Is God angry with me?" He said something like God understood that I had problems. I knew I had to go into the hospital, but deep down I really did not think I would make it out of there. As soon as I got there, I noticed that the sounds I was hearing, my husband was hearing also. When I had gone to the mental hospital in the past, I would be in such a state that I would hear people saying I was going to have a heart attack or noises that no one else would hear, but this time was different. I was not hallucinating. What I was hearing and seeing was real.

We went up to the desk and my husband told them that Dr. King's office had called them. They gave my husband lots of paperwork to fill out and had me sign some papers. One paper I was requested to fill out would be reviewed by the doctor and could allow my release after 24 hours if it was felt I was well enough to go home. If he did not think I could leave, I might have to go to court to see when I could get released. The administrator asked me lots of questions. I told him that over the past few days I had considered overdosing for the ordeal to be over with. I also told him that sometimes I took out my anger on my kids. I had never abused them, but I might snap at them sometimes. I think all mothers have yelled at their children. He then asked me if I wanted to do outpatient therapy, which would take a while to process because they had to get hold of Dr. King's office. I told him I wanted to be admitted because I knew I could not go home in my condition. What was odd was there was no calling of the insurance or waiting for long periods of time, as had been the case on previous admissions. He just took me straight up to the unit. There was no red tape to cut through with the insurance company. At that time I thought it was a little strange that they would need to make calls to Dr. King's office for outpatient treatment but nothing had to be done for inpatient admission.

When I arrived there, Tim, who I remembered from the last time I was there, weighed me. I disliked Tim very much. He was condescending to me and I felt that he did not have my best interests at heart. I was then taken into a room where a nurse asked me a series of questions. I noticed that I could remember things about myself but I was finding it hard to answer questions about my children. I told the nurse that the reason I was there was because I was a selfish person and that I needed to be punished. She said nothing to make me feel better; she just shook her head and left. When I said good-bye to David, he gave me a hug and said, "I am so sorry I have to put you here. You never smoked, did drugs or alcohol or even cursed. This has been a long journey and I am sorry that it is ending."

After he left, I sat down at a table and a black man introduced himself as Randy. He said, "I coordinated this entire hospital visit." I asked, "Is this hell?" He replied, "Yes." He told me he was a drunk and an alcoholic. Who was this guy Randy? Why was he trying to get inside my head? I then went to my room and tried to lie down. After a while I got a roommate, whose name was Emily. I asked Emily, "Why are you here?" She responded, "Because I am a bad person." I felt like she was trying to get inside my head. My head was consumed with all sorts of thoughts, like if I was going to pick a hell, maybe I should have stayed at my house, but I could not do that to the family. She started to crack her knuckles and pace back and forth in the room. She would follow me wherever I went. Whenever she cracked her knuckles it felt like my soul was being beaten up. I felt pain throughout my whole body. Around 6:00, there was visitation, but according to the paper they gave me, there was not supposed to be visitation on Monday night. Lots of patients got visitors. It was really strange. My mom then called and asked, "Isn't David coming to visit?" I explained to her that he just dropped me off and that he was not coming. I did not understand why there was visitation that first night when really there should not have been any. I tried not to let it bother me. I stayed away from phones. I had a huge fear of trying to call home and not being able to get through. I mean it would be terrible if you were stuck in a mental hospital and could not contact anyone. This was one of my fears. When my family called, I would talk to them, but I was not going to call them.

The first night was horrible. I was in excruciating pain and could not sleep. Each minute felt like an hour as I tossed and turned. I asked the nurse for a sleeping pill and she acted like I was bothering her. She finally did as I asked and told me, "Take the damn pill." I told her I did not want it. Emily was hanging around my bed. I said, "Give it to her. I do not want it." The nurse said that Emily got something different than me. I do not know how I made it through that first night, but somehow I did.

On Tuesday, December 30, Tim woke me up and said the doctor would see me then. I felt drugged and very tired. I was seeing a Dr. Camden today since Dr. Mira was on vacation. Dr. Camden asked me if I had an advance directive and I told him no. I told him I was going to be there forever and that I was dead. To me it was like he was hearing my thoughts in my mind, but I was not talking. All I could hear was laughter and noises outside the office door. He abruptly ended the meeting. There was a patient named Latisha who really bothered me. It seemed to me that she purposely said things to make me upset. Tonight was visitation, to which I was looking forward. I was not sure if anybody was going to come. At 6:00 David and Carrie, my sister-in-law, came. I was so excited to see David. I really was not sure if I was ever going to see him again. The visitation went as well as could be expected.

On Wednesday, December 31, I woke up and was in a lot of pain. I could barely walk. I told the nurses I was in pain, and they replied, "Yes, we know." The nurses took no action to help me. To me it seemed some of the patients were evil and out to get me. Along with Randy, there was Kara, who said things like, "There are no doctors here." I would wait in line for food and one of the patients would say other people are waiting. I would take a bite of food and Kara would say, "Finally," like finally she took a bite of food. Latisha would make conversations that did not make sense. She told me she lived just down the street at the corner of Brandy and Wine (like the alcohol). She seemed like a cruel person. I would do a lot of crying and wondering why I was getting punished this severely. What had I done to deserve this? There was no visitation that night. This was the worst New Year's Eve ever.

Lora Bell

After breakfast I would follow the person that brought food and my heart would beat out of my chest and I would feel cold air. The food guy stopped me and asked me what my name was. I told him Lora, and he said, "I love you Lora," and he and a nurse walked me back to my room. The minutes felt like hours, and each minute my body was in excruciating pain. There were no groups or journaling time. I truly felt like I was in my hell on earth, or some other type of hell. Kara had said, "The water is mixed with alcohol." A little after breakfast, I saw a new doctor named Dr. Flint. He told me he knew my doctor, Dr King, and that he was a "round guy." He demonstrated this by putting his arms out in a circular motion. I asked him if I was in hell and he replied. "Yes." I told him that I was hearing noises and he replied, "They were putting in a new boiler." What kind of doctor tells a patient you are in hell and that the stress center is putting in a new boiler? Where was I? I remember going to my room and praying that it would just end. I prayed the Our Father prayer over and over again and it seemed to help some. I would not drink or eat anything because I saw it in my mind as a temptation. I prayed the Hail Mary, and I remember the phone ringing and the person that answered yelled out, "Is there a Mary here?" It was like someone was trying to tell me that praying to Mary was not helping. Finally, a black male nurse came in and asked me what was going on. I told him I thought I was dead and that I was praying for my soul. He replied by saying, "If you are dead, why do you continue to pray?" I did not know how to respond. I just said, "That is a good question." He said, "Well, even though you think you are dead, we are here to make your stay as comfortable as possible."

Later on, I came out of my room and Randy wanted to talk to me. He said, "There must be a lot of things going on in your head and you must have many questions." As I was talking to Randy, I felt like I was going to throw up. Randy tried to convince me that I had taken some medicine to take the edge off, referring to the anti-anxiety medicine, and that I had overdosed. I said it was not true, and that I knew I had not taken too much medicine. He somehow knew that I was in the psychiatric ward when I was pregnant with Katie, my first child, and he was trying to convince me that I had no children. He was trying to put thoughts in my mind that I never had any children. He said, "What I see in you is a lonely person." Randy then made the phone ring the first time. It was my husband, who was urging me to let all my feelings out and to talk to someone there. The conversation seemed like one we had before and I did not believe it. I tried not to believe what was happening. Next, Randy made the phone ring and it was my sister-in-law. Again I just wanted to get off the phone. Then I talked to my brother, who forgot Shelly's name; once again I tried to appear as though these conversations did not affect me. I do not know who Randy was for sure, but I had an idea about for whom he worked.

After I talked to Randy, I tried to lie down. Then, a few minutes later, someone came in saying there was going to be a group. I was surprised because this was only the second group that they had offered since I had been at the hospital. After the group session, I asked to take my medicine, but the nurse did not really want to give it to me. I then tried to lie down again but could not sleep. I got up and noticed a nurse sitting outside a patient's door. The patient Beth, who was inside, was very sick and throwing up. I approached the nurse and asked if Beth was okay, and she told me to go back to bed.

In the front room, a lot of the patients were watching a movie. It was a movie I had never seen before. There was a line in the movie that said something like they are going to lock her up and throw away the key. I asked one of the nurses, "What, are you going to arrest me?" As soon as I said that, the nurse said, "That is it. Turn off the television. Everyone has to go to bed." He said he did not like it, but we had to follow the rules. He added, "I know everyone does not like it, but that is the way it has to be." It was like it was my fault everyone had to go to bed. I went to my room and tried my best to sleep. It was very scary because about every hour someone would come with a flashlight and check to see if I was sleeping.

The next day was Thursday, January 1. I do not really remember much from that day except that a new patient arrived, whose name was Molly. She said she was there because she had blacked out and wrecked her car. To this day I still do not know why they would not do a MRI on her head and instead send her to the stress center. At lunch, I sat down with Molly and Latisha and their conversations made no sense. I even said to Latisha, "You're not making any sense," and she replied, "Yes, I know." Latisha continued to insist that she lived on the corner of Brandy and Wine, like the alcohol. She also told me that she never wanted to leave the stress center. I think it was because she did not have anywhere to go. She also said she worked for St. Thomas More Hospital. Thoughts ran through my mind. Did someone from St. Thomas More Hospital invite her to stay at the stress center to upset other patients like me? What kind of hospital does this?

Today was a visitation day. David, Carrie and my mother-in-law Sue came to visit. They wanted to watch me take my medicine. They said, "Lora, we heard that you refused to take your medicine last night." Actually, the night before I had to ask for my medicine and they really did not want to give it to me. Earlier in the day, I had asked David on the phone to bring me some Blistex. I had been dehydrated from not drinking and my lips were really dry and cracked. He had forgotten the Blistex, which I tried not to let bother me too much. I learned later that the hospital carried Blistex for the patients, but never once did the nurses offer me any. I told myself that, from this day forward, given what had happened to me in here, if I made it out of the hospital, I would join my husband's church, the Church of

Christ. This had been a very awakening experience and I could not go on living my life how I had been. I realized that I had to change the way I lived my life and get baptized and start living my life as a Christian. The first step was to get out of the hospital. During my visit with my family, my husband gave me a picture of my three beautiful daughters. Horrible thoughts of this evil man Randy, who was trying to convince me that I never had any children, entered my mind. I began to think that one day my picture would just vanish or that my children would start disappearing like in the movie "Back to the Future." I felt like I was in a really bad horror movie. I just kept praying that I would get out of there somehow.

The next day was Friday, January 2, and the time was dragging on. I still was not eating that well. On the bright side, I started to make a really good friend, a woman named Jean who was admitted to the hospital with problems similar to mine. She also thought she was dead and had been seeing disturbing images on the television. She had four children and I had three. She was a smoker, but she really wanted to quit. New patients started to arrive and they seemed nicer than those who had been there when I first arrived. I had been in the hospital since Monday the 29th and still had not seen Dr. Mira, my doctor in the hospital. I saw Dr. Camden again that day, but I do not remember going to any group sessions. Every day I prayed that I would have the strength to make it out of the hospital. I did not sleep at all through the night. About every hour someone would come into the room with a flashlight and check to see if I was sleeping. I tried to pretend like I was. I did not want to cause any problems for fear that they would lock me up in a room.

The next day was Saturday, January 3. I thought about my kids a lot that day and wondered how they were doing. I was especially worried about Katie and what she thought had happened to me. I felt terrible that I had let this happen to me again. I really never wanted her to see me in the hospital like this ever again. I was truly worried that I might never see her again or see my little Shelly for her first birthday on January 18th. I actually saw my doctor, Dr Mira, for the first time that day. He seemed a little surprised that I was a patient of Dr. King's. He basically just took notes and asked me questions. He told me to take a shower and to eat. He asked me what had happened to bring me to the hospital and I told him. I explained to him how I was stressed about making Christmas perfect and then I started to feel that I was a selfish person. He just continued to write notes before ending our session.

After everyone had seen the doctor, a social worker named Gloria held a group session. We all took a seat in this little room. Latisha was in there, along with Scott, a new patient. My new friend Jean sat next to me. Molly, the patient who wrecked her car and blacked out, was also there. The group was to pass a ball and answer a question. Gloria explained that she had retired but the hospital kept asking her to come back to help out. When the ball was passed to Scott, he said that he wanted to beat someone up and that he had a lot of anger. He had recently lost his girlfriend and was taking it really hard. I received the ball and was afraid to answer. I finally said that I had low self-esteem. It seemed that everyone in that room was adversely affected by Gloria. She was trying to convince me that I had overdosed on medicine. She was asking me if my husband still supported me and I said, "Yes, of course he does." There was something not right about her, and she made me feel uncomfortable and uneasy.

After the group session, I sat down and thought about the three patients that were at the hospital when I was admitted. First, there was Todd. He had stepped out in front of a car to kill himself. He had sores all over his face. I noticed that he swore a lot. I found out that he had been in the hospital for three weeks with no improvement.

As I was in there with him, I watched in amazement as his sores healed quickly and he became a new person. He told me that he was receiving his medicine and I could tell it was really helping. Why had the nurses not given him his medicine before? All of a sudden he was a changed man. I witnessed this and could not believe it. It was like God gave him a second chance at life. He told me he was a tough guy on the outside, but he was just a cuddly bear on the inside. I really hoped he would take this second chance and live his life differently.

There was another patient named Beth, the one who had been terribly sick on New Year's Eve. I remember that while I was in there with her, there were some days she seemed so sick and depressed and just stayed in her room. She and Todd both mentioned to me that they thought they were in hell. I remember that things started to turn around for Beth. She started to be happier and she was eating. I do not think she had any family. I really felt bad for her because she had some type of mental disability. Her parents probably put her in a home and she was on her own. I could not imagine going through this alone. I am so lucky and blessed to have such a loving and caring family that cared for me. I thanked God every day for that and also for my three beautiful children.

Then there was Jean, the only other person I met with similar symptoms to mine. She and I were becoming close friends. We had a lot in common. We liked the same coffee and we both were good moms who had a little too much stress around the holidays. Her husband went in for a vasectomy and got really sick and was hospitalized. They were also having financial problems around Christmas. She was admitted to St. Thomas More Stress Center about two weeks earlier for the same symptoms but then had to be readmitted again around the same time as me.

There was a newer patient, Matt, who I got along with really well. He said that he was a stay-at-home dad with a 6-month-old and that one day he took out his gun to shoot himself and he dropped the gun. At that moment, his wife rushed to open the door and immediately drove him to the hospital. Matt was the nicest guy and a lot of the patients thought he worked at the hospital because he was helping out with some of the other patients. Matt took to a patient named Frank. Frank had a depressing story. He had a daughter that continued to steal money from him for drugs and he was having a hard time getting away from her and telling her no. Frank also told me that his wife left him to go and find herself. Frank was a really nice old man with a depressing life. I could not help but feel sorry for Frank. On that date we actually started to have groups, and I began making some good friends. I started playing cards with Frank and Matt. I enjoyed our conversations.

Eleven

An End in Sight

The next day, Sunday, was the best day at the hospital yet. That day we had the most group sessions since I was admitted. The groups that day discussed positive thinking. A lot of times I let my thinking control me. I have these terrible thoughts that I am not going to get out of the hospital or that I am dead. I make these thoughts a reality. It is almost like the power of positive thinking, expect it is the power of negative thinking. Once I start with the negative thinking it is very hard for me to stop and start thinking positively. What if your thinking becomes reality? I think it can really happen. If you can positively change your future with positive thinking, then negative thinking can lead to a destructive path. I think my negative thinking was creating my reality. The reality was real and very scary to me. This was the first day at the hospital where we were doing actual groups following a schedule. I was excited because I had visitation with David from 2:30 to 4:00. When he got there, I gave him a big hug. We talked and visited and played some board games. It was really nice to have a long visit with him. While talking with him, I felt like I might actually get out of the hospital soon and that there was actually an end in sight to this whole horrible ordeal.

I continued to make friends, play cards and talk to people. I knew in the back of my mind that some of the staff did not have my best interest at heart. There was a therapist, Tim, who was very condescending towards me. He always seemed to poke fun at me and laugh with his annoying laugh.

On Monday, some more new patients arrived. I personally made it my mission to help out as many patients as I could. I felt like it was my duty to help out in any way possible, because when I came into the hospital I had felt like I was in the process of becoming a very selfish person and I wanted to change that behavior. I know in my heart that David's prayers and the prayers of the members of his church helped me to safely leave the hospital.

I continued to stay in the hospital until Friday, January 10th, when the doctor cleared me to go home. My husband picked me up around 1:30. I said good-bye to all the friends I had made. That day was Jean's 30th birthday, and I wanted to do something for her. When I left the hospital, I went and bought her a card and a couple of cupcakes and left them for her at the entrance to the stress center. I hoped at least this small token helped brighten her day.

When I finally got home, the first thing I heard was "Mommy!" from Rose. It was like music to my ears. I picked up Shelly, my youngest, and she looked at me with her beautiful blue eyes. She gently touched my face and put her thumb in her mouth. I could tell she missed me. It felt great to be home, but I knew it was going to take a little while to get myself into the swing of things. David's dad, John, agreed to stay and help out with me and the kids while David went to work. David and I were greatly appreciative of his help. David's dad has been such a big help to us over the years with my illness that there is nothing that I could do to repay him for all he has done for us. I am so lucky to have such a supportive family.

It took me several weeks to get back to myself and recover from that horrible hospitalization. After going to David's Church of Christ for only about a week, I decided to get baptized. I really felt at the time I had experienced almost a near-death experience in the hospital and it had changed me. Most people would say that I had hallucinated what took place. I did not. These events really happened, and they forced me to examine how I was living my life and how I needed to change it to start living for God. For me this meant no more gambling or drinking, and it also meant going to church three times a week. It has been the best decision I have ever made, and I hope this book will open others' eyes that there is a hell out there. It may be different for everyone, but it does exist. I would remind anyone reading this that they may not be given a second chance like me, and I would urge them to please consider becoming a Christian, getting baptized and joining a Church of Christ. Make the commitment, because we are only on this planet for a short time, but hell is for an eternity. I got a taste of hell and the pain and suffering that is there, and I was very fortunate that I received a second chance. Maybe I received a second chance because I was supposed to write this book and warn everyone that hell exists. Believe me — you do not want to be there. Giving up alcohol and gambling are such small considerations when you think about the greater picture of an eternity in heaven.

Twelve

A Story of Hope

John, David's dad, was very special. He had helped David and me out with my illness over the years, starting back on our honeymoon. He flew down to Cancun to get me out of the hospital and I will never forget the way he helped us out of that situation. When I got out of the hospital this last time in 2009, he came down and stayed with me and the girls while David went back to work. He helped around the house. He did cooking. He was a huge help to David and me. During the day, John and I would play cards and sometimes watch movies. Since my dad died when I was so young, he was kind of like my surrogate father.

Then, shortly after I got out of the hospital in 2009, John was diagnosed with stage 4 lung cancer. The news was devastating to the whole family. We were optimistic, though. He found some good doctors and was going to start treatment. I remember a little while after he was diagnosed, John and I were driving somewhere. I decided to talk to him about the experience I had in the hospital and how it had convinced me to become a Christian. I explained to him that I really thought I had experienced a wake-up call to start living my life differently. He agreed with me that I had witnessed something in there, but he was not convinced that it was the right decision for him. He was content with his current religion and was not ready to be baptized and start living his life as a Christian at that time. I did not feel that I failed in convincing him, only that he was not ready to make that choice at that moment in his life.

John went on to do many more treatments for the lung cancer but nothing seemed to help. The cancer was already in his bloodstream and it was consuming his liver. John refused to give up. No one could ever tell that John was in pain. He never let anyone know. He was a fighter till the end. Then, in September of 2010, he took a turn for the worse. He had a doctor's appointment to see if he could receive oxygen and his vitals did not look good so he was admitted to the hospital.

In the hospital, he got progressively worse. David and I took the kids to visit him while he was still able to talk. We had a nice visit. God must have been with David because he decided to talk with his dad about being baptized. He talked to him and explained to him that he wanted to play baseball with him in heaven. When they were done talking, Sue, David's mom, John and David were all in tears. Now all that had to be decided was where the baptism was going to take place.

The next day, Carrie, my sister-in-law, asked the hospital if they had anywhere to perform a fully immerged baptism. They said they had a therapy bath. It took some time and many people, but we were able to get the baptism set up for the next day. They wheeled John downstairs to the bath area and put him on a stretcher that would be lowered into the water. David would say the words that you believe that Jesus is the only God who takes away the sins, and that "I baptize you to take away the sins." After John came out of the water, he said, "That felt good." Everyone started crying. Then it was almost as though John was at peace. Peace just came over his whole body. It was amazing. Around two in the morning the next day, John passed

Lora Bell

away after his long battle with lung cancer. He will truly be missed. I am so happy to know that he is in heaven and at peace. We know that he is up there because God has sent us a message to let us know. John touched so many lives and some have received a white feather as a message letting them know that he is okay. I truly believe this is God's way of telling us that he is all right and at peace.

Thirteen

Could Satan Contribute to Illness?

My experiences with my mental illness led me to question whether Satan had a hand in my illness. There is much evil and destruction in the world today, so we know that Satan does have a presence here. Why then could he not contribute to illness as well? There is no physical proof of anything wrong with patients' brains that are mentally ill. Doctors say that it is a chemical imbalance in the brain, but can they actually prove that? The truth is that there is no test out there that can demonstrate a chemical imbalance of diagnose this in someone. I had an MRI done on my brain when I was having all of those physical symptoms related to postpartum depression after Rose was born, and the radiologist reported that my brain looked unremarkable. Think of all the murderers behind bars. A lot of them say that Satan told them to kill. Maybe Satan is controlling a lot of these bad seeds. They have probably been delinquent their whole lives and Satan just had some type of control over them. I think it is very possible to fall under Satan's spell. The more bad you do, the more you are under his control. With the types of psychosis that I experienced, I have to wonder if Satan did not contribute to my illness. I am not saying that all illness is caused by Satan, because I think a lot of illness is caused from the environment. My dad died of bladder cancer and the doctors think that his disease was environmental. I definitely think most cancer is caused by the environment or what we put in our bodies. A lot of cancer is caused from smoking, consuming alcohol or drinking too much soda. Maybe a lot a people are just more susceptible to getting cancer than others. We may never know the answers. As for mental illness, it is kind of a mystery because there is no tumor or any real physical cause to the illness. You just have to go on the faith of the psychiatrist that he has the right diagnosis.

I am also not saying that becoming a Christian is going to fix your mental illness. If you have a mental illness, you will still need to take your medicine and to continue to see your doctor. I am just saying that becoming a Christian has helped me. The evil has been taken out of my life. The gambling is gone. I used to gamble a lot, and I felt awful when I lost. My fear of dying is at ease. I am not as frightened as I used to be. I used to be terrified, and now I am not. I remember I used to be afraid to fall asleep at night for fear that I would die in the middle of the night. My fear is much better now. My anxiety level is better. I am a happier and more motivated person. I have a more positive outlook on life now.

Fourteen

What Do You Have To Do To Become A Christian

David has stuck with me since 1997, and sometimes I have to ask myself why. Why didn't he ask for an annulment after my psychosis on our honeymoon? David and I were meant to stay together through these rough times to get to where we are today. I feel confident that after being in the hospital eight times, I will never ever be in another psychiatric ward in the future. I feel that becoming a Christian has helped me solve a lot of my problems with schizoaffective disorder. I do not know that I will ever be able to come off of the medicine completely, but I would eventually, with my doctor's permission, like to greatly reduce my dosage. I do know that I have always had problems with my mood since I was in my teens and early twenties. Sometimes the smallest of situations would bother me and I would cry and get upset. I do know for a fact that I will never have any more hallucinations or psychosis ever again, and that feels good.

To make it to heaven you have to become a Christian. What do you have to do to become a Christian? You have to make sacrifices in your life. If you smoke, you need to quit. Why can't you smoke? The Bible never directly mentions smoking outright, but it does say that we should not allow our bodies to be mastered by anything. 1 Corinthians 6:12 states "Everything is permissible for me," but not everything is beneficial. "Everything is permissible for me," but I will not be mastered by anything. Then verse 19 and 20 states: "Do you not know that your body is a temple of the Holy Spirit, who is in you, whom you have received from God? You are not your own; you were bought at a price. Therefore, honor God with your body." Smoking harms your body and it is addictive, which is considered a sin.

Alcoholism or being addicted to alcohol is a sin and will prevent you from entering heaven. If you use alcohol to get drunk and do not know when to stop, it is a problem. You need to seek treatment before becoming a Christian. Also, the same goes for drug abuse. There are lots of references to alcohol in the bible, some good and some bad. Basically, what it comes down to is a decision you and God have to make. If you feel that you can have a drink every once in a while and you are okay with that and your heart is right with that decision, then more power to you. Personally, I do not drink. My brother is a recovering alcoholic, and I believe my sister struggles with alcohol. I wish I could help her, but she refuses to think she has a problem. Recently, my sister called me on the phone while drunk. I did not know what to say. I just pretended like everything was fine. My only hope is that she will read my book and change her ways and stop drinking. Her drinking is not only hurting her; it is hurting the whole family.

I am the only Christian in my family. My mom, sister and brother are Catholics who do not attend church weekly. I can only hope that this book opens their eyes and that they will make some changes in their life. My ultimate goal would be for them to become Christians, but they are also gamblers.

This brings me to my next topic. Why is gambling a sin? Well, think about it; they don't call Las Vegas "Sin City" for nothing. Gambling can lead to addiction, just like alcohol and drugs can. Also, God commands us to work for what we have, and he will supply for us. The gambler hopes to get money from not working, and then he would quit his job if he ever won big. Before I became a Christian, I used to gamble a lot, especially with my family from Pittsburgh. My brother, sister and mom are all gamblers. I used to love to play blackjack. I was never satisfied with winning a little; I always wanted more. I lost a lot of money gambling, and it caused a strain in my marriage. When I was gambling, it was like a thrill that I just could not get enough of and that is what makes it so evil and dangerous to you and your family life.

To become a Christian is a commitment. It is a commitment to put God first. The first step is to ask for forgiveness for your sins and to tell yourself that you are going to try not to gamble, do drugs, smoke or drink alcohol again. If you do, you can always ask for forgiveness. God always forgives. The next step is to say that you acknowledge that Jesus is the only son of God in front of some witnesses. Then you get baptized. You are fully submerged in water. You then want to try to go to a church whenever they meet. The church I go to meets three times a week — Sunday morning, Sunday night and Wednesday evening. I know it sounds like a lot, but you will meet a lot of good people.

I want to also let you know that no church is perfect. That goes for the Church of Christ also. There will be members of the church who will cheat on their husbands or wives, just like any other church. Sometimes they will be forgiven by their spouse and sometimes not. If their spouse decides not to forgive them, then they will probably divorce. The spouse who did the cheating is never to marry again; this is according to the Bible. The other spouse who was cheated on can find a new spouse. There will also be members who will struggle with other personal demons. I just want to let you know you will still have obstacles to overcome, but hopefully by becoming a Christian you will feel better about who you have become. You will hopefully make some great friends that share your same values.

By writing this book and sharing my experiences I hope I can help at least one person turn their life around and become a Christian. I believe maybe I was given this illness of schizoaffective disorder so I could help others who struggle with mental illness, alcoholism or drug abuse. I know a lot of people are not going to believe what has happened to me, but to me it was a very real experience. I truly believe I was in my own personal hell for about the first four days of my hospital stay at St. Thomas More Stress Center. I made it out with the help of prayers and being strong. I decided to change my life for the better after my experiences. My main objective is to tell you that Satan is real and your hell may be different than your neighbor's, but it does exist. Your time here on earth could be short or long, but you are in heaven or hell for an eternity. What will you decide?

www.ingramcontent.com/pod-product-compliance
Ingram Content Group UK Ltd.
Pitfield, Milton Keynes, MK11 3LW, UK
UKHW041948230426
12048UKWH00008B/206

CAMBRIDGE LIBRARY COLLECTION
Books of enduring scholarly value

Music

The systematic academic study of music gave rise to works of description, analysis and criticism, by composers and performers, philosophers and anthropologists, historians and teachers, and by a new kind of scholar - the musicologist. This series makes available a range of significant works encompassing all aspects of the developing discipline.

Catechism of Musical Aesthetics

One of the most important musicologists of his age, Hugo Riemann (1849-1919) influenced an entire generation in its thinking. He held several teaching posts before settling at the University of Leipzig in 1895. A prolific writer on music theory, publishing works on almost every aspect of the subject, he is best remembered for his celebrated *Musik-Lexikon* (1882). These three lectures, setting out his thinking on how we listen to music, were first published in 1888 as *Wie hören wir Musik?* and in 1895 in this English translation by Heinrich Bewerunge (1862-1923), plainchant scholar at St Patrick's College, Maynooth. Each lecture deals with a different aspect of the overarching question posed in the original title, revealing Riemann's thoughts on the transformation of hearing into feeling, the different psychological effects of dynamics, emotional responses to rhythm and harmony, and passive and active listening.

Cambridge University Press has long been a pioneer in the reissuing of out-of-print titles from its own backlist, producing digital reprints of books that are still sought after by scholars and students but could not be reprinted economically using traditional technology. The Cambridge Library Collection extends this activity to a wider range of books which are still of importance to researchers and professionals, either for the source material they contain, or as landmarks in the history of their academic discipline.

Drawing from the world-renowned collections in the Cambridge University Library and other partner libraries, and guided by the advice of experts in each subject area, Cambridge University Press is using state-of-the-art scanning machines in its own Printing House to capture the content of each book selected for inclusion. The files are processed to give a consistently clear, crisp image, and the books finished to the high quality standard for which the Press is recognised around the world. The latest print-on-demand technology ensures that the books will remain available indefinitely, and that orders for single or multiple copies can quickly be supplied.

The Cambridge Library Collection brings back to life books of enduring scholarly value (including out-of-copyright works originally issued by other publishers) across a wide range of disciplines in the humanities and social sciences and in science and technology.